THE INDIAN MYTHICAL CREATURES

AN EXPLORATION OF INDIA'S FOLKLORE AND MYTHICAL CREATURES

DR. JAGADEESH PILLAI

Made with ♥ on the Notion Press Platform
www.notionpress.com

|| Dedicated to all wisdom seekers around the World ||

Contents

Contents

Prayer

**"Om Bhadram Karnebhih Shrunuyaama
DevaahBhadram Pashyemaakshabhiryajatraah
SthirairangaistushtuvaamsastanoobhihVyashema
Devahitam YadaayuhSwasti Na Indro
VridhashravaahSwasti Nah Pooshaa
VishwavedaahSwasti Nastaarkshyo ArishtanemihSwasti
No Brihaspatir DadhaatuOm Shantih, Shantih, Shantih"**

The literal meaning of this mantra is: OM. O Gods! Let us
hear auspicious words from our ears. O reverent Gods! Let
us behold propitious visions from our eyes, let our organs
and body be stable, healthy, and strong. Let us do that
which is pleasing to the gods in the life span allotted to us.
May Indra, inscribed in the scriptures, bring us fortune!
May Pushan, the knower of the world, grant us prosperity!
May Trakshya, who vanquishes enemies, bestow us with
blessings! May Brihaspati bring us success!
OM Peace, Peace, Peace.

About The Author

Dr. Jagadeesh Pillai is a renowned Guinness World Record holder, writer, and researcher hailing from Varanasi, also known as the abode of Lord Shiva. With a Ph.D. in Vedic Science and a range of creative ideas and achievements, he is a true polymath. He is the author of more than 100 books including Research Publications. Although his roots can be traced back to Kerala, the people of Varanasi hold him in high regard and affectionately consider him one of their own.

In 1998, Dr. Pillai was offered a job at Banaras Hindu University, but he left the position after only two months to pursue greater goals in life. He believed that in order to study Indian scriptures and engage in other creative endeavours, he needed to retire from the daily grind of working solely for money at a young age.

He started an export business from scratch, using the knowledge he had gained from a previous job in the industry. His intelligence and unique approach to business led to great success in a short period of time, earning him more in just a decade and a half than he would have in a lifetime working in a government job. Upon the passing of Dr. APJ Abdul Kalam, Dr. Pillai decided to leave the business and dedicate himself to reading, studying, researching, and experimenting.

During his tenure in the export business, Dr. Pillai traveled to over 16 countries, gaining valuable insight and experiencing the world and life in detail.

Dr. Pillai has achieved four Guinness World Records in the following subjects:

"Script to Screen" - In this record, Dr. Pillai produced and directed an animation film within the shortest time possible, breaking the previous record set by Canadians. He has also received numerous national and international awards and recognitions for this achievement.

Longest Line of Postcards - For this record, Dr. Pillai created a line of 16,300 postcards on the occasion of the 163rd anniversary of Indian Postal Day. The event also included a questionnaire about the Indian flag.

Largest Poster Awareness Campaign - Dr. Pillai designed an awareness campaign on the subject of "Beti Bachao - Beti Padhao" (Save the Girl Child - Educate the Girl Child) to achieve this record.

Largest Envelope - In tribute to the Indian Prime Minister's "Make in India" initiative, Dr. Pillai created a 4000 square meter envelope using waste paper to achieve this record.

Attempted - **70000 Candles on a 210 kg Cake** - To celebrate the 70th Indian Independence Day, Dr. Pillai attempted to light 70,000 candles on a 210 kg cake, which was recorded in World Records India.

Attempted - **Documentary on Dhamek Stupa of Sarnath in 17 Languages** - Dr. Pillai attempted to create a documentary on the Dhamek Stupa of Sarnath, dubbing it in 17 different languages. The result of this attempt is currently awaiting confirmation from the Guinness World Records.

Dr. Pillai is skilled in teaching the Bhagavad Gita, a Hindu scripture, and is popular among young people. He has helped many young people improve their lives through his motivational teachings.

In addition to teaching, he has composed and sung numerous Sanskrit Bhajans and patriotic songs.

He has also written and directed several short films and documentaries for awareness campaigns, and has volunteered with the police in both UP and Kerala to spread awareness about various issues through videos and photography.

Incredibly, he has produced and directed over 100 documentaries about the city of Varanasi, all on his own.

He has also helped and guided more than 25 boys and girls to achieve world records through creative and innovative methods. He is a multifaceted person who uses his intellect and the blessings given to him by God to excel in various areas. He is both a teacher and a student, always learning and teaching, and is able to master any subject he comes across.

He is a selfless social activist and motivational speaker who has overcome struggles and failures to become a successful and enthusiastic individual with a rich life experience.

In addition to his work with the Bhagavad Gita, he is also an efficient Tarot card reader, Astro-Vastu consultant, and a talented singer and composer. He has sung the entire Ram Charita Manas and Bhagavad Gita in his own compositions, and has sung the phrase "Lokah Samastha Sukhino Bhavantu" in 50 different languages. He is currently working on a detailed and scientific study of Vedas, Upanishads, Puranas, and the Bhagavad Gita. He has also composed and sung the Hanuman Chalisa and Gayatri Mantra in 108 and 1008 different compositions, respectively.

Awards - Four Times Guinness World Records, Winner of Mahatma Gandhi Vishwa Shanti Puraskar, Mahatma Gandhi Global Peace Ambassador, Kashi Ratna Award, Dr. APJ Abdul Kalam Motivational Person of the Year 2017, Mother Teresa Award, Indira Gandhi Priyadarshini Award, Bharat Vikas Ratna Award, Udyog Ratna Award, Vigyan Prasar Award, Poorvanchal Ratn Samman.

PREFACE

In this book, "The Indian Mythical Creatures: An Exploration of India's Folklore and Mythical Creatures," readers will be taken on a journey through the fascinating world of Indian mythology. From the ancient gods and goddesses to the mysterious creatures that inhabit the land, this book will explore the rich and varied folklore of India.

From the majestic Garuda to the mischievous Pishacha, readers will discover the unique and captivating creatures that have been part of Indian culture for centuries. Through vivid descriptions and engaging stories, this book will bring to life the mythical creatures of India and the stories that surround them.

In addition to exploring the creatures of Indian mythology, this book will also delve into the history and culture of India. From the ancient Vedic texts to the modern-day interpretations of Indian mythology, readers will gain a deeper understanding of the country's rich and diverse culture.

This book is an essential guide for anyone interested in learning more about India's mythical creatures and the stories that surround them. With its captivating tales and vivid descriptions, this book will provide readers with an unforgettable journey through the magical world of Indian mythology.

I

Introduction to the Indian Mythical Creatures

India is a land of rich culture and mythology, and its mythical creatures have been a source of fascination for centuries. From the benevolent gods of the Hindu pantheon to the mischievous yakshas of Buddhist lore, these creatures have captivated the imaginations of people around the world. In this chapter, we will explore the fascinating world of Indian mythical creatures, delving into their origins, characteristics, and roles in Indian folklore.

The gods of the Hindu pantheon are perhaps the most well-known of India's mythical creatures. These gods are often depicted as having human-like forms, but with superhuman powers. They are responsible for maintaining the balance of the universe and are often associated with natural phenomena such as rain, thunder, and lightning.

The most popular gods include Brahma, Vishnu, and Shiva, who are often depicted in Hindu art and literature.

The yakshas are another type of mythical creature found in Indian mythology. These creatures are often depicted as mischievous and playful, and are often associated with wealth and prosperity. They are often depicted as having human-like forms, but with animal features such as horns, wings, and tails. Yakshas are often associated with water and are believed to inhabit rivers, lakes, and other bodies of water.

The rakshasas are another type of mythical creature found in Indian mythology. These creatures are often depicted as evil and dangerous, and are often associated with chaos and destruction. They are often depicted as having human-like forms, but with animal features such as horns, wings, and tails. Rakshasas are often associated with darkness and are believed to inhabit forests and other dark places.

The nagas are another type of mythical creature found in Indian mythology. These creatures are often depicted as wise and powerful, and are often associated with knowledge and wisdom. They are often depicted as having human-like forms, but with serpentine features such as scales and a tail. Nagas are also associated with water and are often depicted as living in rivers, lakes, and oceans. They are also believed to possess magical powers and are sometimes depicted as protectors of treasure. Unlike rakshasas, nagas are often depicted as benevolent and helpful, rather than evil and dangerous.

ॐ

"The rich folklore of India's mythical
creatures is a source of inspiration for artists
and storytellers alike."

৩

II

Ancient Indian Myths and Legends

India is a land steeped in ancient myths and legends, with stories of gods, goddesses, and mythical creatures that have been passed down through generations. From the powerful Garuda, the eagle-like bird of Hindu mythology, to the mischievous Yakshas, the nature spirits of Buddhism, India's mythical creatures have captivated the imaginations of people for centuries.

The Garuda is one of the most iconic mythical creatures in India. It is said to be the mount of Vishnu, the Hindu god of preservation, and is often depicted as a large bird with a human-like face. In Hindu mythology, the Garuda is a symbol of strength and courage, and is said to be able to fly at incredible speeds.

The Yakshas are another popular mythical creature in India. They are nature spirits that are said to inhabit forests and mountains, and are often depicted as mischievous tricksters. In Buddhist mythology, the Yakshas are said to be protectors of the Dharma, or the teachings of the Buddha.

The Naga is a mythical serpent-like creature that is said to inhabit the rivers and oceans of India. In Hindu mythology, the Naga is a symbol of fertility and prosperity, and is often depicted as a large snake with multiple heads. In Buddhist mythology, the Naga is said to be a protector of the Dharma, and is often depicted as a large snake with a human-like face.

The Rakshasa is a mythical creature that is said to inhabit the forests of India. In Hindu mythology, the Rakshasa is a symbol of evil and chaos, and is often depicted as a large, humanoid creature with sharp claws and fangs. In Buddhist mythology, the Rakshasa is a type of demon that is said to feed on human flesh and is often depicted as a large, humanoid creature with animal features such as horns, wings, and tails. Rakshasas are often associated with darkness and are believed to have the ability to shape-shift into various forms, making them difficult to detect and defeat. Despite their evil nature, some Hindu texts describe Rakshasas as having the ability to attain salvation and become benevolent beings, and some even depict them as loyal servants of the gods.

"In Indian folklore, mythical creatures hold a
special place as protectors of nature and
wildlife."

༚

III

The Naga: Serpentine Beings with Divine Powers

The Naga are a mysterious race of serpentine beings that have been part of Indian folklore for centuries. They are said to possess divine powers and are often depicted as half-human, half-serpent creatures. In Hindu mythology, they are believed to be guardians of the underworld and protectors of sacred waters.

The Naga are often associated with fertility and abundance, and are believed to bring good luck and prosperity to those who honor them. They are also said to be able to grant wishes and provide guidance to those who seek it. In some stories, they are even said to be able to transform into human form and interact with people.

The Naga are often depicted as having multiple heads,

ranging from two to a hundred. They are usually depicted as having a human torso and a serpentine tail. They are often associated with water, and are said to live in rivers, lakes, and oceans.

The Naga are also said to be able to control the weather and bring rain. They are also believed to be able to bring fertility to the land and protect it from harm. In some stories, they are even said to be able to bring the dead back to life.

The Naga are an important part of Indian mythology and folklore, and are often seen as powerful and benevolent beings. They are believed to be able to bring good luck, prosperity, and guidance to those who honor them. They are also said to be able to protect the land from harm and bring fertility and abundance to those who seek it.

"The mythical creatures of India are a symbol of the country's diverse and rich spiritual traditions."

ॐ

IV

The Kinnara: Heavenly Musicians

The Kinnara are a unique breed of mythical creature found in Indian folklore. They are described as having the body of a human and the head of a horse, and are said to be the most beautiful of all the mythical creatures. They are also known for their musical prowess, playing a variety of instruments such as the flute, lute, and drums.

The Kinnara are said to live in the heavenly realms, where they play music for the gods and goddesses. They are also said to be the guardians of the sacred rivers, protecting them from harm.

The Kinnara are often depicted in Hindu art and literature, and are said to be the source of inspiration for many of India's greatest musicians. They are also said to be the source of the divine music that is heard in the heavens.

The Kinnara are said to be the messengers of the gods, and are believed to bring good luck and fortune to those who hear their music. They are also said to be the protectors of the sacred rivers, and are believed to bring peace and harmony to those who listen to their music.

The Kinnara are said to be the embodiment of beauty and grace, and are often seen as a symbol of divine love and harmony. They are also said to be the source of inspiration for many of India's greatest musicians, and are believed to bring joy and happiness to those who hear their music.

The Kinnara are a unique and fascinating part of Indian folklore, and their music is said to bring peace and harmony to those who listen. They are a symbol of divine love and harmony, and are believed to bring good luck and fortune to those who hear their music.

"The stories of Indian mythical creatures
have captivated the imagination of
generations and continue to do so today."

❧

V
Airavat: The Celestial Elephant

Airavat, the celestial elephant, is a powerful figure in Indian mythology. He is the mount of the Hindu god Indra, the king of the gods, and is said to have four tusks and a white body. He is often depicted with a white lotus in his trunk, symbolizing purity and divine power.

Airavat is said to have been born from the churning of the cosmic ocean, and is believed to have the power to bring rain and fertility to the land. He is also said to be the guardian of the four directions, and is often seen as a symbol of strength and protection.

In Hindu mythology, Airavat is also associated with the sun god, Surya. He is said to have been created from the rays of the sun, and is believed to be the source of all life. He is also said to be the protector of the gods, and is often seen as a symbol of divine power and protection.

Airavat is also associated with the goddess Lakshmi, the goddess of wealth and prosperity. He is said to bring good luck and fortune to those who worship him. He is also said to be the guardian of the four directions, and is often seen as a symbol of strength and protection.

Airavat is a powerful figure in Indian mythology, and is seen as a symbol of strength, protection, and divine power. He is said to bring rain and fertility to the land, and is believed to be the source of all life. He is also associated with the sun god, Surya, and the goddess Lakshmi, and is seen as a symbol of good luck and fortune. Airavat is a powerful figure in Indian mythology, and is sure to bring blessings and prosperity to those who honor and worship him.

In Hindu mythology, Airavat is depicted as a large and magnificent elephant, often with multiple heads, and is considered to be one of the eight celestial elephants who carry the world on their backs. He is also said to have the ability to control the winds, and is associated with the Hindu god of rain and thunder, Indra. In some Hindu texts, Airavat is also described as the king of all elephants, and is said to have been born from the churning of the ocean of milk.

Overall, Airavat holds a significant place in Indian mythology and is seen as a symbol of prosperity, strength, and protection. He is revered by Hindu followers and is often invoked for blessings and protection in Hindu rituals and ceremonies.

"In Indian mythology, mythical creatures
serve as guardians of the natural world and
its elements."

℗

VI

The Vetala: Vampiric Spirits

The Vetala, also known as the Baital, is a vampiric spirit from Indian folklore. It is said to inhabit the corpses of humans and animals, and is known for its mischievous and often malicious behavior. It is believed to be able to possess the living, and is said to be able to take on the form of a human or animal.

The Vetala is said to be able to speak and understand human language, and is known for its intelligence and cunning. It is said to be able to answer questions posed to it, and is often sought out by those seeking knowledge or advice. It is also said to be able to grant wishes, though it is often said to do so in a way that is not beneficial to the wisher.

The Vetala is said to be able to cause harm to humans, and is often blamed for illnesses and other misfortunes. It is said to be able to cause nightmares, and is said to be able to possess the living and cause them to do its bidding. It is also said to be able to cause death, and is often blamed for sudden and unexpected deaths.

The Vetala is said to be able to be defeated by those who are brave and knowledgeable. It is said that those who are able to outwit the Vetala will be rewarded with knowledge and power. It is also said that those who are able to defeat the Vetala will be able to gain control over it, and will be able to use it to their advantage.

The Vetala is a powerful and mysterious creature from Indian folklore, and is said to be able to cause both harm and good. It is a creature that is both feared and respected, and is said to possess knowledge of secrets and hidden truths. The Vetala is typically depicted as a supernatural being that inhabits the bodies of dead people and is able to manipulate them. In Hindu mythology, it is considered a type of demon, but it is also said to have the ability to grant wishes and bestow knowledge upon those who are able to defeat it in a test of wit. The Vetala is a popular figure in Indian folklore and continues to be the subject of many tales and legends.

"The depiction of mythical creatures in
Indian art and literature is a testament to
the country's rich cultural heritage."

৪৩

VII

The Pishacha: Ghosts and Demons

The Pishacha are a type of ghostly creature found in Indian mythology. They are said to be the spirits of those who have died a violent death, and are believed to haunt the living. They are described as having a human-like form, with a head that is half-human and half-animal, and a body covered in fur. They are said to be able to take on different shapes and sizes, and can even possess humans.

The Pishacha are said to be able to cause great harm to humans, and are often blamed for illnesses and misfortunes. They are said to be able to cause nightmares, and can even drive people to insanity. They are also said to be able to possess humans, and can cause them to do evil deeds.

The Pishacha are said to be able to be appeased by offerings of food and drink, and by performing rituals. They are also said to be able to be driven away by the chanting of mantras and the burning of incense.

In some stories, the Pishacha are said to be able to grant wishes to those who are brave enough to ask them. However, these wishes often come with a price, and can have dire consequences.

The Pishacha are a fascinating part of Indian mythology, and their stories have been passed down through generations. They are a reminder of the power of the supernatural, and the dangers that lurk in the shadows. They are a reminder that even in the modern world, there are still things that we do not understand, and that we should be wary of.

The Pishacha are often depicted as malevolent spirits that feed on the fear and suffering of humans. They are said to be particularly active at night, and are believed to possess immense powers that can cause harm to those who cross their path. In Hindu mythology, they are considered to be the offspring of the demon king, Rahu, and are said to have a taste for human flesh.

Despite their reputation as malevolent creatures, there are some stories in which the Pishacha are portrayed in a more positive light. In these tales, they are seen as powerful beings who are capable of granting wishes to those who are brave enough to ask them. However, as mentioned, these wishes often come with a price, and can have dire consequences.

The Pishacha are often associated with death and destruction, and are considered to be a symbol of the darker aspects of the supernatural. However, they also play an important role in the Hindu pantheon, serving as a reminder of the balance of power between good and evil.

The Pishacha are an integral part of Indian folklore, and their stories continue to captivate and terrify people to this day. They serve as a reminder of the power of the supernatural and the dangers that it poses to humanity, and are a testament to the enduring power of mythology and legend.

"The mythical creatures of India are a representation of the country's diverse spiritual beliefs and cultural traditions."

౬౩

VIII

Chakora: The Moon-loving Bird

Chakora is a mythical bird found in Indian folklore. It is said to be a bird that loves the moon and is often associated with the lunar cycle. It is believed to be a symbol of purity and devotion, and is often used to represent the power of love and faithfulness.

The Chakora is described as a small bird with a white body and a black head. It is said to have a long, curved beak and a long tail. It is believed to be a nocturnal creature, and is often seen flying around the moon at night.

The Chakora is said to be a very loyal bird, and it is believed that it will never leave its mate. It is also said to be a very wise creature, and it is believed that it can understand the language of humans.

The Chakora is said to be a very powerful creature, and

it is believed that it can bring good luck and fortune to those who are devoted to it. It is also said to be a symbol of fertility and abundance, and it is believed that it can bring prosperity and abundance to those who are devoted to it.

The Chakora is a beloved creature in Indian folklore, and it is often used in stories and songs to represent the power of love and faithfulness. It is a symbol of purity and devotion, and it is believed to bring good luck and fortune to those who are devoted to it.

The Chakora is said to feed on the light of the moon, and is often depicted as a bird-like creature with delicate features and a pure white complexion. It is said to possess a strong connection to the moon, and is believed to be able to grant wishes and provide guidance to those who are devoted to it.

In Hindu mythology, the Chakora is considered to be a sacred creature, and is often associated with the goddess Chandra, the goddess of the moon. It is said that those who are able to please Chandra by feeding the Chakora will be blessed with good luck, fortune, and prosperity.

The Chakora is also an important symbol in Indian literature, and is often used to represent the power of love and devotion. It is said that a Chakora will only appear in the presence of a person who is pure of heart and true in their love and devotion.

The Chakora is a revered creature in Indian folklore, and its stories and symbolism continue to inspire and captivate people to this day. It is a symbol of the power of love and devotion, and is believed to bring good luck, fortune, and prosperity to those who are devoted to it.

"The rich folklore of India's mythical creatures offers a glimpse into the country's cultural and spiritual history."

☙

IX

The Yali: Lion-like Creatures with Tusks

The Yali is a mythical creature found in Indian folklore and mythology. It is described as a lion-like creature with tusks, and is often depicted as a guardian of temples and other sacred places. It is said to have the power to protect its domain from evil forces and to bring good luck to those who worship it.

The Yali is believed to have originated in the Hindu epic, the Ramayana. In the epic, the Yali is described as a powerful creature that is able to defeat the demon king Ravana. It is also said to have been the mount of the god Vishnu.

The Yali is often depicted in Hindu art and sculpture, and is a popular subject in Indian folk tales. It is said to have the power to grant wishes and to bring good luck to those who worship it. It is also believed to be a symbol of strength and courage.

The Yali is also associated with the Hindu goddess Durga. She is said to have ridden a Yali during her battle with the demon Mahishasura. The Yali is also said to have been the mount of the god Shiva.

The Yali is a popular figure in Indian culture and is often used as a symbol of strength and courage. It is believed to bring good luck and protection to those who worship it. It is also said to be a guardian of temples and other sacred places.

The Yali is a powerful and mysterious creature that has been a part of Indian folklore and mythology for centuries. It is a symbol of strength, courage, and protection, and is said to bring good luck to those who worship it. It is a popular figure in Hindu art and sculpture, and is often depicted as a mythical creature with the body of a lion and the head of a demon. It is said to possess immense strength and power, and is considered to be a fierce protector of the innocent.

In Hindu mythology, the Yali is said to be a powerful demon who was defeated by the god Vishnu. Despite its demonic origins, the Yali is often portrayed as a benevolent creature, and is said to protect temples and other sacred places. It is also said to bring good luck and fortune to those who worship it, and is considered to be a powerful guardian and protector.

The Yali is also an important symbol in Indian architecture, and is often depicted as a decorative element on temples and other sacred buildings. Its image is used to symbolize strength, power, and protection, and is meant to evoke feelings of security and stability.

The Yali is a powerful and enduring symbol in Indian culture, and its stories and mythology continue to inspire and captivate people to this day. It is a symbol of strength, courage, and protection, and is said to bring good luck and fortune to those who worship it.

"In Indian folklore, mythical creatures serve
as a connection between the physical and
spiritual realms."

ॐ

X

The Apsaras: Heavenly Dancers and Enchantresses

The Apsaras are a captivating part of India's folklore and mythology. These celestial beings are said to be the most beautiful of all the mythical creatures, with their graceful movements and enchanting beauty. They are often depicted as female dancers, with long flowing hair and delicate features.

The Apsaras are said to be the daughters of the gods, sent down to earth to entertain and enchant the gods and humans alike. They are said to be able to take on any form they desire, from birds to animals, and even humans. They are also said to be able to fly, and often appear in the sky, dancing and singing.

The Apsaras are said to be able to use their beauty and

charm to influence humans and gods alike. They are said to be able to use their powers to bring good luck and fortune, or to bring misfortune and bad luck. They are also said to be able to use their powers to bring love and harmony, or to cause discord and strife.

The Apsaras are said to be able to use their powers to bring about change in the world, and to help shape the destiny of humans and gods alike. They are said to be able to use their powers to bring about peace and prosperity, or to bring about chaos and destruction.

The Apsaras are said to be able to use their powers to bring about justice and fairness, or to bring about injustice and unfairness. They are said to be able to use their powers to bring about harmony and balance, or to bring about disharmony and imbalance.

The Apsaras are said to be able to use their powers to bring about good fortune and luck, or to bring about misfortune and bad luck. They are believed to have the ability to influence human affairs and are associated with the Hindu pantheon of gods and goddesses. They are often depicted as celestial nymphs and are associated with water, fertility, and beauty.

"The stories of Indian mythical creatures
have been passed down for centuries, keeping
their cultural and spiritual significance
alive."

જી

XI

Makara: The Sea Monster

Makara is a mythical creature that has been part of Indian folklore for centuries. It is described as a hybrid creature, with the head of an elephant, the body of a fish, and the tail of a crocodile. It is often depicted as a guardian of the sea, protecting the waters from evil forces.

In Hindu mythology, Makara is associated with the god Varuna, the god of the sea. It is believed that Makara is the vehicle of Varuna, and that it is capable of traversing both the physical and spiritual realms. Makara is also associated with the god Ganesha, who is often depicted riding on its back.

Makara is also a symbol of fertility and abundance. In Hindu mythology, it is believed that Makara is the source of all life, and that it is responsible for the abundance of the seas. It is also believed to be a symbol of good luck and prosperity.

In Indian art, Makara is often depicted as a powerful and majestic creature. It is often shown with its trunk raised, as if it is ready to protect the waters from any danger. It is also often shown with its tail raised, as if it is ready to take flight.

Makara is a powerful symbol in Indian culture, and it is often used to represent strength, courage, and protection. It is a reminder of the power of the sea, and of the importance of protecting the environment. It is also a reminder of the importance of respecting the natural world and its creatures.

In Hindu mythology, Makara is considered as the mount or vehicle of the river goddess Ganga and the sea god Varuna. It is also depicted as the companion of the Hindu god of wisdom and wealth, Lord Ganesha. Makara is also associated with astrological signs and is considered to be the zodiac sign for Capricorn.

In Indian art, Makara is often depicted in various forms including as a sea monster, a fish, or a combination of both. It is also commonly depicted in sculptures and carvings as a decorative element in temples, palaces, and other buildings.

The depiction of Makara as a fierce protector and symbol of strength has made it a popular emblem in various forms of art, such as paintings, textiles, and jewelry. It is also used as a symbol of good luck and prosperity and is commonly found in Indian homes and places of worship.

Makara holds a special place in Indian culture and art,

representing power, protection, and respect for nature. Its depiction in various forms continues to inspire and remind people of the importance of preserving the natural world and its creatures.

"The mythical creatures of India are a
symbol of the country's rich and diverse
cultural heritage."

೫

XII

The Rakshasa: Demon-like Creatures with Supernatural Powers

The Rakshasa are a powerful and feared race of supernatural creatures found in Indian mythology. They are often depicted as demonic, with sharp claws, fangs, and a thirst for human flesh. They possess a variety of supernatural powers, including the ability to shape-shift, fly, and cast powerful spells.

Rakshasas are said to be the children of the Hindu god Brahma, and are believed to be the guardians of the underworld. They are often seen as the enemies of the gods, and are said to be responsible for many of the misfortunes that befall mortals.

Rakshasas are also known for their cunning and intelligence. They are said to be able to outwit even the most powerful of gods, and are often seen as the ultimate tricksters. They are also known for their ability to manipulate and deceive humans, often using their shape-shifting powers to disguise themselves as humans in order to gain access to their victims.

Rakshasas are also said to be able to control the elements, and are often seen as the bringers of storms and other natural disasters. They are also said to be able to control the minds of humans, and are often seen as the cause of madness and insanity.

The Rakshasa are a powerful and feared race of supernatural creatures, and their presence in Indian mythology is undeniable. They are often seen as the ultimate tricksters, and their ability to manipulate and deceive humans is legendary. They are also said to be able to control the elements, and are often seen as the bringers of storms and other natural disasters. The Rakshasa are a powerful force to be reckoned with, and their presence in Indian mythology is both fascinating and frightening.

In Hindu mythology, Rakshasas are portrayed as evil and malevolent beings who prey on humans and cause chaos and destruction. They are said to have the power to change their appearance, and can appear as beautiful or as ugly, depending on their needs. They are also said to have immense physical strength and the ability to control the minds of humans.

Despite their fearsome reputation, Rakshasas are also depicted as cunning and intelligent, able to outwit humans with their tricks and illusions. They are often portrayed as antagonists in Hindu epics and stories, but they are also seen as protectors of dharma or righteousness.

In Hindu religion, Rakshasas are associated with the night, and are said to roam the earth during the hours of darkness. They are also associated with the planet Mars and the Hindu god of death and destruction, Lord Shiva.

Rakshasas are a complex and multi-faceted part of Indian mythology, embodying both fear and admiration. Their depiction as powerful and cunning supernatural creatures continues to captivate and inspire the imagination of people in India and beyond.

*"In Indian mythology, mythical creatures
serve as protectors of the land and its people."*

ॐ

XIII

Navagunjara: The Beast with Many Heads

Navagunjara is a creature of Indian mythology, described as having the head of a rooster, the neck of a peacock, the back of a bull, the waist of a lion, the thighs of a wild goat, and the feet of a tiger. It is said to have been created by the gods to protect the world from evil.

Navagunjara is a powerful creature, possessing immense strength and agility. It is said to be able to move swiftly and silently, and to be able to traverse any terrain with ease. Its many heads are said to be able to see in all directions, allowing it to detect danger from any angle.

Navagunjara is also said to possess magical powers, such as the ability to transform into any creature it desires. It is said to be able to use its many heads to create illusions, and to be able to control the elements.

Navagunjara is a symbol of protection and strength in Indian mythology. It is said to be a guardian of the gods, and to be able to protect the world from evil. It is also said to be a symbol of unity, as its many heads represent the many different cultures and religions of India.

Navagunjara is a fascinating creature of Indian mythology, and its many heads and magical powers make it a powerful symbol of protection and strength. It is a creature that has been revered for centuries, and its legacy continues to live on in the stories and legends of India.

Navagunjara is often depicted as a mystical being with the head of a rooster, the body of a deer, the arms of an elephant, the trunk of a wild boar, and the legs of a lion and an ox. This combination of parts from different animals symbolizes the unity and integration of different cultures and traditions in India.

In Hindu mythology, Navagunjara is said to have been created by the Hindu god Lord Vishnu to protect the world from evil and to maintain balance and harmony. It is also said to be able to control the elements and to have the ability to bring rain and fertility to the land.

Navagunjara is also associated with astrology and is believed to be the ninth sign of the Hindu zodiac. It is considered to be a powerful symbol of protection and is often invoked in Hindu prayers and rituals to ward off evil and bring good fortune.

In Indian art, Navagunjara is often depicted in sculptures and carvings, and it continues to be a popular subject of Hindu folklore and storytelling. Its depiction as a symbol of protection and unity has made it a beloved part of Indian culture and heritage.

Navagunjara holds a special place in Indian mythology, embodying the ideals of protection, unity, and balance. Its depiction as a powerful and mystical creature continues to inspire and captivate people in India and beyond.

"The depiction of mythical creatures in Indian art and literature showcases the country's rich creative and spiritual traditions."

ॐ

XIV

The Yaksha: Nature Spirits and Guardians of Treasure

The Yaksha are a mysterious and powerful race of nature spirits found in Indian folklore. They are often depicted as powerful guardians of hidden treasures, and are said to be able to shape-shift into various forms. They are also known to be fierce protectors of nature, and are said to be able to control the elements.

The Yaksha are believed to have originated in the Vedic period, and are mentioned in the Rigveda, the oldest of the four Vedas. They are described as powerful and mysterious beings, and are said to be able to grant boons to those who seek their help.

The Yaksha are also associated with the god Kubera, who is said to be their king. Kubera is often depicted as a wealthy and powerful figure, and is said to be the guardian of all wealth and treasures. He is also said to be the guardian of the Yaksha, and is often depicted as riding a chariot pulled by eight Yaksha.

The Yaksha are also associated with the god Yama, the god of death. Yama is said to be the ruler of the Yaksha, and is often depicted as riding a chariot pulled by eight Yaksha. He is also said to be the guardian of the underworld, and is said to be able to grant boons to those who seek his help.

The Yaksha are also associated with the goddess Lakshmi, the goddess of wealth and prosperity. Lakshmi is said to be the consort of Kubera, and is often depicted as riding a chariot pulled by eight Yaksha. She is said to be the guardian of wealth and prosperity, and is said to be able to grant boons to those who seek her help.

In Hindu mythology, Yakshas are depicted as benevolent and powerful supernatural beings who inhabit the earth, the sky, and the underworld. They are said to be protectors of the earth, and are often associated with nature, fertility, and wealth. Yakshas are also depicted as guardians of treasures and are said to be able to grant boons to those who seek their help.

Yakshas are depicted in many different forms in Indian art and mythology, ranging from fierce and powerful creatures to gentle and nurturing beings. They are often depicted as human-like figures, with some having animal-like features such as tusks or horns.

In Hindu religion, Yakshas are associated with the planet Mercury and the Hindu god of wealth, Kubera. They are also associated with the Hindu god of death, Yama, and are said to be his faithful servants.

Yakshas hold an important place in Indian mythology as benevolent and powerful supernatural beings associated with nature, wealth, and protection. Their depiction as guardians of the earth, treasure, and the underworld has made them a fascinating and enduring part of Indian culture and heritage.

"The rich folklore of India's mythical creatures is a testament to the country's imagination and cultural heritage."

ℭ

XV

The Wendigo and Wechuge: Spirits of the North

The Wendigo and Wechuge are two of the most feared and revered spirits of the North. Both are said to be powerful and mysterious, with the ability to shape-shift and take on different forms. The Wendigo is a malevolent spirit, often associated with cannibalism and violence, while the Wechuge is a benevolent spirit, associated with healing and protection.

The Wendigo is said to be a tall, gaunt figure with glowing eyes and long, sharp claws. It is said to be able to take on the form of a human, an animal, or even a tree. It is believed to be a spirit of the wilderness, and is often associated with winter and cold weather. It is said to be able to possess humans, and is believed to be the cause of many cases of cannibalism.

The Wechuge is said to be a benevolent spirit, associated with healing and protection. It is said to be able to take on the form of a human, an animal, or even a tree. It is believed to be a spirit of the wilderness, and is often associated with summer and warm weather. It is said to be able to possess humans, and is believed to be the cause of many cases of healing and protection.

The Wendigo and Wechuge are two of the most mysterious and powerful spirits of the North. They are said to be able to shape-shift and take on different forms, and are believed to be able to possess humans. They are often associated with winter and summer, respectively, and are believed to be the cause of many cases of cannibalism and healing. They are both feared and revered, and are an integral part of the traditional beliefs of many indigenous communities in the North.

The Wendigo and Wechuge are often depicted as powerful spirits that have the ability to control the elements and have the power to bring both good and bad luck. They are often associated with winter and summer, and are said to bring either famine or abundance, depending on the season.

In indigenous beliefs, the Wendigo is often seen as a symbol of starvation and is believed to be responsible for bringing harsh winters and famine. It is also associated with cannibalism and is said to possess humans and make them engage in such acts.

On the other hand, the Wechuge is seen as a spirit of healing and protection, and is believed to bring warm weather and abundance. It is often associated with the natural world and is believed to be a spirit of the wilderness.

The Wendigo and Wechuge hold a significant place in the beliefs and traditions of indigenous communities in the North. They are powerful spirits that are associated with the elements and are believed to bring either good or bad luck, depending on the season. These spirits continue to be revered and respected, and their influence remains a significant part of the spiritual beliefs of indigenous people to this day.

"The mythical creatures of India are a representation of the country's diverse spiritual beliefs and cultural customs"

॰

XVI

The Bhuta: Haunted Beings and Specters

The Bhuta are a type of supernatural creature found in Indian folklore. They are often described as ghostly figures, with a variety of shapes and sizes. They are said to haunt places such as abandoned buildings, graveyards, and forests.

The Bhuta are believed to be the spirits of people who have died in tragic circumstances, such as murder or suicide. They are said to be filled with rage and sorrow, and seek revenge on those who wronged them in life. They are also said to be able to possess people, causing them to act in strange and unpredictable ways.

The Bhuta are often seen as a warning sign of impending danger. People who encounter them are said to be in danger of being cursed or attacked. It is believed that the Bhuta can be appeased by offerings of food and flowers, or by performing rituals to ward them off.

The Bhuta are also said to be able to grant wishes, although this is a risky endeavor. It is said that if the Bhuta are not appeased, they can become angry and cause harm to those who have made the request.

The Bhuta are a fascinating part of Indian folklore, and their stories have been passed down through generations. They are a reminder of the power of the supernatural, and the importance of respecting the dead.

They are also a symbol of the delicate balance between the living and the dead, and a cautionary tale of the consequences of neglecting the spirits of the afterlife. Whether seen as a source of blessings or a harbinger of harm, the Bhuta play a central role in the beliefs and traditions of India.

"The stories of Indian mythical creatures are not just legends, but hold important cultural and spiritual meanings."

୫

XVII

N-Dam-Keno-Wet: The Giant Water Monster

N-Dam-Keno-Wet is a giant water monster that has been part of Indian folklore for centuries. It is said to inhabit the depths of the Indian Ocean, and is described as a giant serpent-like creature with a long, scaly body and a head resembling that of a dragon. It is said to be able to create huge waves and whirlpools, and is capable of swallowing ships whole.

The legend of N-Dam-Keno-Wet is believed to have originated in the ancient Hindu scriptures, where it is described as a powerful creature that can bring destruction and chaos to the world. It is said to be the guardian of the ocean, and is believed to be the source of all the storms and floods that occur in the Indian Ocean.

The creature is also said to be able to control the weather, and is believed to be responsible for the monsoon rains that occur in India. It is also said to be able to cause earthquakes and tsunamis, and is believed to be the cause of many of the natural disasters that have occurred in India over the centuries.

N-Dam-Keno-Wet is a powerful and feared creature in Indian mythology, and is often invoked in prayers and rituals to protect against natural disasters. It is also believed to be a symbol of strength and power, and is often used as a symbol of protection in Hindu temples.

The legend of N-Dam-Keno-Wet has been passed down through generations, and is still a part of Indian culture today. It is a powerful symbol of the power of nature, and a reminder of the importance of respecting and protecting the environment.

N-Dam-Keno-Wet is a mythical creature that is revered in many parts of India, and its legacy continues to live on through various prayers, rituals and cultural practices. Despite being a symbol of fear and destruction, it is also seen as a symbol of protection and is invoked to prevent harm to the community and the environment. The story of N-Dam-Keno-Wet serves as a reminder of the power of nature and the need to respect and maintain balance in the ecosystem.

"The depiction of mythical creatures in
Indian art and literature showcases the
country's rich creative heritage."

☙

XVIII

Thunderbirds: Mystic Birds with Powerful Wings

The Thunderbird is a powerful creature of Indian folklore, with wings that can create thunder and lightning. It is said to be a giant bird, larger than any other bird in the world, with a wingspan that can reach up to 10 feet. Its feathers are said to be made of pure gold, and its eyes are said to be so bright that they can blind anyone who looks into them.

The Thunderbird is said to be a protector of the land, and it is believed that it can bring rain and fertility to the land. It is also said to be a symbol of strength and power, and it is believed that it can ward off evil spirits and protect people from danger.

The Thunderbird is also said to be a messenger of the gods, and it is believed that it can bring messages from the gods to the people. It is also said to be a symbol of good luck, and it is believed that it can bring good fortune to those who encounter it.

The Thunderbird is a powerful creature, and it is said to be able to fly faster than any other bird in the world. It is also said to be able to create storms and lightning, and it is believed that it can control the weather. It is also said to be able to bring rain and fertility to the land, and it is believed that it can bring good luck to those who encounter it.

The Thunderbird is a powerful creature of Indian folklore, and it is said to be a symbol of strength, power, and good luck. It is believed to be a protector of the land, a messenger of the gods, and a bringer of rain and fertility. It is a powerful creature that can create storms and lightning, and it is said to be able to control the weather. The Thunderbird is a revered and respected creature in Indian mythology, and its legacy continues to live on in the beliefs and traditions of the people.

"In Indian mythology, mythical creatures
serve as messengers between the gods and
humans."

છ

XIX

The Garuda: The Mighty Eagle

The Garuda is a powerful figure in Indian mythology, often depicted as a large bird with a human-like face. It is said to be the mount of the Hindu god Vishnu, and is often seen as a symbol of strength and courage. In some stories, the Garuda is said to be the son of the sage Kashyapa and his wife Vinata, and is described as having a golden body, a white face, and a beak of iron.

The Garuda is said to be the enemy of the Nagas, a race of serpent-like creatures in Hindu mythology. In some stories, the Garuda is said to have been sent by Vishnu to steal the Amrita, the elixir of immortality, from the Nagas. In other stories, the Garuda is said to have been sent by Vishnu to rescue his devotee, the sage Markandeya, from the clutches of the Nagas.

The Garuda is also said to be the protector of the Hindu

gods, and is often seen as a symbol of protection and strength. In some stories, the Garuda is said to have been sent by Vishnu to protect the gods from the demons. In other stories, the Garuda is said to have been sent by Vishnu to protect the gods from the Asuras, a race of powerful demons.

The Garuda is also said to be the messenger of the gods, and is often seen as a symbol of communication and intelligence. In some stories, the Garuda is said to have been sent by Vishnu to deliver messages to the gods. In other stories, the Garuda is said to have been sent by Vishnu to bring news of important events to the gods. The Garuda is also seen as a symbol of courage and selflessness, as it is said to have performed various acts of bravery to protect the gods and help preserve the balance of the universe. Overall, the Garuda is a revered and powerful figure in Hindu mythology, and continues to be an important symbol in Indian culture and religion.

"The mythical creatures of India are a
representation of the country's cultural and
spiritual beliefs."

౭౩

XX

Skinwalkers: Humanoid Shapeshifters

Skinwalkers are a type of humanoid shapeshifter found in the folklore of many Native American tribes. They are believed to be able to transform into any animal they choose, and are often associated with dark magic and evil deeds.

The origin of skinwalkers is shrouded in mystery, with some believing they are the result of a curse placed upon a person by a powerful shaman. Others believe they are the result of a person being possessed by a spirit, or that they are the result of a person making a pact with a dark entity. Whatever the origin, skinwalkers are feared by many Native Americans, and are often seen as a sign of bad luck.

Skinwalkers are said to have the ability to transform into

any animal they choose, and can even take on the form of a human. They are said to be able to move quickly and silently, and can even fly. They are also said to have supernatural powers, such as the ability to control the weather and to cause illness.

Skinwalkers are often seen as a threat to humans, as they are believed to be able to cause harm to people and animals. They are also said to be able to steal the souls of their victims, and to be able to possess people. In some stories, skinwalkers are said to be able to transform into a wolf or a coyote, and to be able to use their powers to hunt and kill humans.

Skinwalkers are a fascinating part of Native American folklore, and have been the subject of many stories and legends. They are often seen as a symbol of fear and danger, but also as a symbol of power and strength. They are a reminder of the mysterious and powerful forces that exist in the world, and of the importance of respecting the natural order of things.

Skinwalkers are a well-known and intriguing aspect of Native American folklore. The beliefs and stories surrounding skinwalkers vary among different indigenous cultures, but they are generally seen as malevolent beings with the ability to shape-shift into animals and cause harm to people and animals. They are often associated with magic, supernatural abilities, and evil intentions, and are a reminder of the darker aspects of the natural world.

"The tales of Indian mythical creatures offer a glimpse into the country's rich cultural history."

"India's folklore and mythical creatures are a captivating exploration of the unknown."

"The Indian mythical creatures are a fascinating window into the culture and history of India."

"The mythical creatures of India are a testament to the country's rich and vibrant culture."

"The Indian mythical creatures are a source of wonder and amazement, full of mystery and intrigue."

"The Indian mythical creatures are a reminder of the power of imagination and creativity."

"The Indian mythical creatures are a unique and captivating part of India's cultural heritage."

"The Indian mythical creatures are a testament to the country's rich and diverse mythology."

"The Indian mythical creatures are a source of inspiration and awe, full of mystery and enchantment."

"The Indian mythical creatures are a reminder of the beauty and complexity of India's culture and history."

"The Indian mythical creatures are a fascinating exploration of the unknown, full of mystery and wonder."

"The Indian mythical creatures are a source of enchantment and mystery, full of imagination and creativity."

"The Indian mythical creatures are a unique and captivating part of India's cultural identity."

"The Indian mythical creatures are a reminder of the power of the imagination and the beauty of India's culture."

"The Indian mythical creatures are a captivating exploration of India's folklore and mythology."

"The Indian mythical creatures are a source of wonder and amazement, full of mystery and intrigue."

"India's mythical creatures are a reflection of its rich cultural heritage and imagination."

"Each creature in Indian folklore has its own unique story and symbolism."

"The diversity of India's mythical creatures is a testament to its diverse culture."

"In Indian mythology, mythical creatures serve as both protectors and antagonists."

"The mythical creatures of India are an integral part of its history and mythology."

"The stories of Indian mythical creatures have been passed down through generations, keeping their legacy alive."

"The diversity of Indian mythical creatures is a reflection of the country's diverse geography and climate."

"In Indian folklore, mythical creatures serve as a bridge between the natural and supernatural worlds."

"The mythical creatures of India are a symbol of the country's rich spiritual traditions."

"India's mythical creatures are a part of its rich and colorful cultural tapestry."

***

Other Books Of The Author

1. The Moments When I Met God
2. Kashiyile Theertha Pathangal
3. GURU GYAN VANI
4. Abhiprerak Gita
5. ASSI SE JAIN GHAT TAK
6. Hopelessness of Arjuna
7. The Soul and It's True Nature
8. Sense of Action (Karma)
9. Action through Wisdom
10. Action through Wisdom
11. THEORY AND PRACTICAL OF EVERY ACTION
12. LOGICAL UNDERSTANDING OF THE SUPREME
13. THE IMPERISHABLE SUPREME
14. Yatra Nishadraj se Hanuman Ghat Tak
15. Yatra Karnatak Ghat se Raja Ghat Tak
16. Yatra Pandey Ghat se Prayagraj Ghat Tak
17. Yatra Ranjendra Prasad Ghat se Dattatreya Ghat Tak
18. YaatraSindhiya Ghat se Gwaliar Ghat Tak
19. Yatra Mangala Gauri Ghat se Hanuman Gadhi Ghat Tak
20. Yatra Gaay Ghat Se Nishad Ghat Tak
21. MAA GANGA, GHATEN EVM UTSAV
22. Ganga Arti Dev Deepavali evam Any Utsav
23. Potentials of Digitalized India
24. VEDIC CONSCIOUSNESS
25. A Brief Introduction to Vedic Science
26. Kashi ke Barah Jyotirling
27. IMPACT OF MOTIVATION
28. Let's have a Milky Way Journey
29. Color Therapy in a Nutshell

30. Rigveda in a Nutshell
31. Yajurveda in a Nutshell
32. Samveda in a Nutshell
33. Atharva Veda in a Nutshell
34. Ayushman Bhava - Ayurveda
35. Srimad Bhagavad Gita and Upanishad Connection
36. Srimad Bhagavad Gita - an attempt to summarize each chapter.
37. Facts and Impact of Nakshatra
38. Astro Gems - NAVARATNA
39. Ekadashi - A Concise Overview
40. A Concise View of Hanuman Chalisa
41. Inspirational Gita
42. Nakshatraranyam
43. Summary of 18 Mahapuranas
44. Synopsis of 18 Upa Puranas
45. Rigvediya Upanishads
46. Shukla Yajurvediya Upanishads
47. Krishna Yajurvediya Upanishads
48. Samavediya Upanishads
49. Atharvavediya Upanishads
50. The Seven Great Sages
51. From Rocket Scientist to President Dr. APJ Abdul Kalam
52. The Visionary's Voice - Quotes of Dr. APJ Abdul Kalam
53. The Wisdom of Swami Vivekananda: Insights and Inspiration from a Legendary Spiritual Teacher
54. Ayurvedic Remedies from the Garden
55. Sages and Seers
56. Rising Strong – Motivational Stories of Women
57. Beyond Flames -Mystery stories of Funeral Ghat Manikarnika
58. The Origins of Tulsi: A Look at the Mythological Roots of the Plant"

121. Innovative Startups - 25 Startup Ideas to Spark Your Business Creativity
122. Export Management: Strategies for Global Success
123. Exporting from India - A Step by Step Guide
124. Finance Fundamentals: Mastering Financial Management for Business Success
125. Global Growth Strategies for International Business Development
126. Marketing Mastery: Unlocking the Secrets of Modern Marketing
127. Operations Mastery: Managing the Flow of Value in Business
128. Strategic Business Management: Navigating the Modern Business Landscape
129. Human Resource Management Strategies for Building and Managing a High Performance Team
130. The Indian Landscapes and Nature: An Exploration Of India's Natural Beauty And Diversity
131. The Indian Street Performances: A Cultural Exploration of India's Street Performances
132. Affirming Your Self-Worth: Strategies for Achieving Emotional Wellbeing
133. Cultivating Self-Discipline: Secrets Methods for Achieving Your Goals
134. Embracing Change: Strategies for Adapting to Life's Challenges
135. Embracing Your Uniqueness: Secret Strategies for Living an Authentic Life
136. Finding Motivation in Despondency: Coping with Difficult Times
137. Embracing Change
138. Learning to Love Yourself
139. Managing Time for Yourself

Contact

DR. JAGADEESH PILLAI

MBA & PhD in Vedic Science

Four Times Guinness World Record Holder

Winner of Mahatma Gandhi Vishwa Shanti Puraskar and
Global Peace Ambassador

Gemology, Astro & Vastu Consultant - Spiritual Counselor

Consultant for designing World Record Ideas

Efficient Tarot Card Reader

9839093003

myrichindia@gmail.com

drjagadeeshpillai@facebook

drjagadeeshpillai@instagram
jagadeeshpillai@youtube

www. JAGADEESHPILLAI.com

|| LOKAHA SAMASTHAHA SUKHINO BHAVANTU ||